Waves of a Raining Mind

POEMS

Mohamed Bangura

Sierra Leonean Writers Series

Waves of a Raining Mind

Copyright © 2016 by Mohamed Bangura
All rights reserved.

No part of this book may be reproduced in any form or by any electronic or mechanical means except by reviewers for the public press without written permission from the author and/or the publishers.

ISBN: 978-99910-54-73-5

Sierra Leonean Writers Series

DEDICATION

This book of poetry is dedicated to my family, colleagues, lovers of poetry, my former and present students

An Introduction

By

Abdulai Walon-Jalloh

Author of
- *Voices and Passions* (SLWS 2015 - Poems)
- *Hungry Vultures (*SLWS 2016 – A Play*)*
- Lectures Syntax in the Linguistics Unit Department of Language Studies, Fourah Bay College, University of Sierra Leone.

This debut collection by **Mohamed Bangura** is a very loaded piece that deals with garbage and regeneration as evident in **THE PULSE OF KROOBAY** in which he keeps the reader puzzled in wonderment and fear with regards the murky ambience that reeks to the firmament though Mohamed inspires the atmosphere with the 'hen' and 'chick' grace against a backdrop of 'beauty'. Our fears continue because even 'beauty' will 'prostrate to splendor flames.' However a 'trace' of 'sunrise' will continue to uplift the mood. The excesses of the human condition are heightened by 'passion crimes'. On the other hand, Mohamed in **DUNIA** portrays a determined persona who is struggling between action and inertia, achievements and failure and hopes and an unfulfilled existence. The poet Mohamed dabbles with the high promise of higher learning and the frolicking leisure of the Lumley – Aberdeen coast line. Furthermore, In the poem **FREETOWN ABERDEEN WHARF** Mohamed continues to engage with the elements and the human condition in all their vibrancy and awe. The sea-shore represents finality and regeneration. This contrast exerts an exciting ambience which the reader will hardly miss. Mohamed's allusion to the 'Sapes', one of the oldest inhabitants of the Sierra Leone coastline, evokes a very strong sense of going back.

This journey back into the past is an attempt at juggling the present for the future in a bid to enter the future with confidence and knowledge of who we truly are. 'Aberdeen Wharf' is home to 'meteors ocean toys' and also the genesis of the first 'Sapes algae'. Mohamed, further, delves into **THE MORNING BIRD'S SONG** which is an intense engagement with nature during the early hours of dawn. A reluctant but eager-eyed persona is seemingly woken up by a 'creaking firefly', the 'torch' that is 'flocking the sofa' and the not-to be subdued 'Azan's welcome pry'. The morning is 'foggy' with the Harmattan' and 'the cloudy silver linen'. The foggy and cloudy environments are direct representatives of the persona's inner torment. The bird song is normally meant to uplift the spirits but here it is doing the opposite. The 'shaky office joy' does not do the trick either because the persona is beset with promises and counter promises as evidenced in 'Incessant sad hope / Of change smeared dope'. **LINES TO APOST-EBOLA POET** is a tribute to an emerging post-ebola poet Abdulai Walon-Jalloh the author of *Voices and Passions*. The persona assures the reader he the persona will continue to 'listens'. Walon-Jalloh's diction is characterized as capable of leading us to the 'path of sublime lyrics' 'with that taunt of poetic nesting' the latter offering us the opportunity 'to escape the chant spirit debasing'. The getaway idea is very vivid in the first stanza and the punch of the lines cannot be missed. The piece manifests a strong idea of resilience and protest as evidenced in 'of pure discipline the heart to imagery sting / cheering meekly this dust that follows his wind / where secret spurs felt the sojourned mind'. **WRITER'S BLOCK** brings to the fore the inability of writers to sometimes continue to be creative. The block readily sends the 'right hemisphere' of the brain on vacation.

THE FERRY THAT BROUGHT ME by Mohamed Bangura opens with a stanza that harps on slavery and demeaning poverty as evidenced by 'distance penury', 'stench slums' and 'suffering hills'. This time-travel piece evokes a sense of longing and connection because the persona is 'not stripped of ... reflection' and is able to overcome barriers by being able to acknowledge the trials and grasp the tiny embers of hope. The 'ferry' itself is a metaphor. **THE BEACH WAVES** evokes the elements and mirror them against the human condition. The changing tidal waves are synonymous with the vicissitudes of life. We mortals have little or no control over our destinies. **IN SEARCH OF MY TEENAGE LOVE** paints a sense of 'burning desires ... down memory lane'. 'Maria' symbolizes yearning and unrequited love. **COMMON ROOM COMRADES** or rather still **COMMON COMRADES** is a joyous poem with an elevated sense of place and time. The first stanza is an epitome of fulfilment after a long drawn out struggle to acquire education at the Mountain of Hope Fourah Bay College. The journey has been one likened to a 'trail of an ant linked in migratory birds' choir'. The piece recalls the nostalgia of 'wisdom Tree' and the glamour of 'Bustik'. Mohamed displays his craftsmanship adroitly and vividly in the **SWIMMING FISH** with its sudden visual and kinaesthetic encounters between the persona and the 'fish' and the persona and the 'woman girly' which are not accidental. In **HOMECOMING** or **COMING BACK FROM THE DIASPORA** which reminds the reader of Lenrie Peters' *WE HAVE COME HOME*. He is a poet possessed by haste and didactics. He proselytizes in vain because the African over the centuries has been preconditioned to believe not in himself and to always run to the former colonial masters in both times of plenty and want. Mohamed however makes use of contrasts and synecdoche to capture the two opposing worlds. **HYSTERIA** is a nature-filled poem that paints a landscape of animation and pensiveness. The reader is taken through a plain of 'grassy field, 'dizzy squirrels', 'jabbering parrots', 'yawning pens' and 'winking ... lids' to prove the evidence of adventure and excitement and transition. The night is characterized by 'light' going 'off', 'vehicles and cars tiring pass' and gates being locked. It is like a state of suspended animation. **MORE TIME ON THE STOOL** reveals a puzzle that is exercising the mind of the persona. The conundrum regarding 'more time on the stool' permeates the poem. The persona hopes for a divine or super intervention but I think he will be disappointed because change is effected by men, brave men. 'Freedom' and 'justice' do not come easily to the undeserving. **I WILL BECOME A CHILD AGAIN** is a beauty of motherhood and childhood all combined to give one strong effect of the days of innocence and caring. **LOVE LATECOMER** represents the philosophical musings in this twelve line verse of speed, hesitancy, symbolism and conciseness. The bestiality can be passed off even with the dress up. However, 'emotion' is kept at 'bay'. **DREAM** represents a reverie since the persona appears to be wide awake. The three stanza poems details a transitional phase in the life of the persona from the time of the 'devil silence' during his slumber to the time he warned of his 'belongings' not to be taken away. A smooth transition is observed in line three of the first stanza and in the penultimate line in stanza three. **TUTORS** the poem traverses the world of the teachers and journalists. It reminds one of the profound sacrifices the two categories of professionals make to a society. **TO MY POETRY MENTOR** is an ode-like poem in all its sincere and sustained noble sentiments done in dignified and appropriate style though lacking the musical quality associated with poems in this category. The poetry mentor though imagined has inspired the persona. The persona sees his poetry as 'naked'. The persona prays for the mentor.

KENEMA is a poem of praise, place, time and longing. The piece is very sharp or pointed because it brings to live the eastern city, Kenema. **THE KALAHARI** is another of those pieces that details a sense of place, time and longing just like KENEMA. **ON THE GRAVE OF A WAR HERO** paints a contrasting picture of events. The piece displays a canvass of life in which the 'lions and hyenas play', leopards tickle their peers', fox and elephants sleep, monkeys sing and spiders built their stunning mansions'. This is what has become of the war hero. **THE HARMATTAN** is a piece that engages with the power of the dry 'Harmattan' that ravishes Sierra Leone December and February. This period in Sierra Leone is so dry and cold that the 'vaseline' and 'blanket' are of little use. Our 'lips and skin' will be dry from the cold dry wind that will blow from 'Targrin' especially for the Western Area Urban. However, the 'sun' will come to our rescue. Furthermore, the persona will deploy 'stockings and jackets'. **THE FIRST SUN OF THE DRY SEASON** is celebratory piece that welcomes the Dry Season one of the two major seasons in Sierra Leone. It is normally that time of the year when plants will die and ready to grow again. Mohamed uses the camaraderie of 'Ataya base' to serve as a convergence point that will anchor the activities of the poem. Young people love 'Ataya base cocoon' but it gives them the opportunity to be free, expressive and resistant as expressed in 'last man standing'. **FOURAH BAY COLLEGE LIBRARY** focuses on the persona's forays at the library of Fourah Bay College during his quest for knowledge. The persona is surprised to be at the library especially considering the amount of time spent going through 'index cards'. This piece amongst other things reminds us about the triumph of the human spirit over adverse conditions. **THE HOUSE IN THE FOREST** is a celebratory piece in honour of the 'forest'. All the elements ('sun', 'rain', 'wind' and 'night', are connected with the 'forest'. Living things like 'animals', 'owners' and 'hunters' are dependent on goodwill of the forest. Mohamed brilliantly deploys the images and symbols to bring the 'forest' alive in all its majestic splendour. **DISTANT SCHOLAR** paints a picture of an aspiring being that happens to be at the pinnacle of success. The persona acknowledges the goodwill of humanity towards him and is grateful especially to the 'mount that made crumbs'. This makes the piece very gratifying indeed. **BEAUTIFUL ORCHARD** is a philosophical poem in which the persona muses about strong and compelling desire that ranges from intense sensual and sexual love to non-platonic asexual love. We are amazed at his bravery though worried about his foolishness, as well. The persona triumphs because we are informed that there is a 're-echo' of stories over gossip. The persona when he beholds 'fireflies' he becomes 'motionless'. This inertia is not cause by actual fire flies but by the overwhelming powers of love. The 'orchard' as we all know is a beautiful place that inspires warmth and sweet sensations and this is exactly what the poet wants us to experience. **THE MYTH COTTON TREE** is a dazzling piece on the power of the 'Cotton Tree' both in historical and contemporary times. The tree has come to represent a point for bonding and acknowledgement of unity. Mohamed has penned down a cultural classic imbued with a sense of history, myth and tradition. **LAUGHTER** is a joy-inspiring piece similar to George Coleridge-Taylor's *Tintern Abbey*. 'Laughter' can serve as a 'taunter' and is capable of romancing 'humanity'. **EDUCATION**, traces the definitive power of education and implicitly the lack of it thereof. 'Education' is seen as the 'sculptor', the 'key', 'manual' and 'way to righteousness'. This piece is very simple to understand because it is not laden with complex denseness and philosophical exposes. Mohamed is at his most direct compare to his other poem in his debut collection. **THE CLASSROOM IS MOTHER** celebrates the importance of the 'classroom'. The metaphor is never lost on the reader because the reader is aware of the seminal nature of formal knowledge processes. Mohamed's craftsmanship comes alive in the final lines of the last stanza. The times spent in the 'classroom' is not wasted because it helps the persona to be at ease in the present and there is a longing for that time spent in the 'classroom'. There is the desire for classroom or knowledge to be in abundance just like the 'nation's pacific'. **SUNSET ON THE SHORE** paints a beautiful picture of nature, adventurism and social night out. 'Sunset' beholds the 'beaming' 'ocean liner' that 'crosses the cunning Bay' as the 'wailing market shields' 'a deserted field'. We see 'curved canoes' braving the ocean and their wares will dot the 'wealthy pile of fins dandling faces' to the delight of those ashore. The time cited by the persona holds a mixed bag of jollying, feasting and daring. This piece is dense and symbolic and just as Boagey (1977) affirms artists normally hide their craft and critics will find the craft. Mohamed on this note has not failed us. Again, the poem is a dazzling beauty of visual and motion juxtaposed at the setting of the sun. **THE GRASS AND I** is a philosophical poem that touches on the nature of beings. The 'grass' and 'cradle' represent our demise and regeneration as living things. The 'rabbit' and 'I' represents the commonality of the species and also their brilliance on this earth. There is a stark warning for the youth here referred to as the 'child' who seems to be toying with 'the aged rough' but is also consoling the 'bickering cradle'. **WOMAN STAND UP** focuses on the condition of the woman over the centuries. He cleverly rallies men and women to action by invoking the classical women of yester and present times. 'Madam Yoko' and 'Ella Koblo Gulama' are two notable and legendary women of the (19th and (20th centuries in the history of Sierra Leone. On the other hand, **PITY** is an example of those subverting pieces that instruct by inverting the pyramid. 'Pity' or self-pity is something we all wallow in and would to continue doing. However, Mohamed fights this menace by inspiring us to 'shout' our 'hearts high'. The persona further inspires us to 'swim' our 'lap' in order to 'save the last clap' for the persona. This piece challenges us to be stoics like the Spartans of ancient times. No matter our condition we must never give in to desolation and 'pity'. **WHY BLAME ME?** is a defiant, arrogant and boastful piece. On the other hand it portrays a persona that is above reproach. This is unacceptable because there is no perfect individual. **DRUMS BORN AGAIN** touches on the age-old topic of religion and traditional cultural practices like the masquerades and other secret societies. The 'drums' represent the crier who will marshal everyone interested to the dance floors or secluded bushes to perform the rituals of the masquerade. **THE MEMORY VALLEY** evokes a sense of eternal bliss as embodied in the concept of heaven in indirect manner. **THE EXCESSES OF POLITICS** is a protest piece that sees very little positives in the game of 'politics'. Mohamed is very open and comes through vividly. His anger is unmasked and there is little pretence in the message. **IGNORANCE** celebrates the power of information and knowledge. The piece decries ignorance and goes on further to state the consequences of being ignorant. **WAITING TIME** provides the reader the idea of time not waiting for anyone. Time spent is time lost and cannot be regained. **ASK FOR IT?** starts off with a question that will serve as a refrain and opening for all the stanzas. This largely unanswered refrain heightens the atmosphere or tension in the piece. We are reminded that whatever we ask for will be within reach or grasp because the 'week comes with it', 'it is sold just now' and comes with 'honey cream'. **BEGGARS** the poem reveals the ordeals of beggars who have to stand, push, rush, sit and crawl. **WHAT ARE WE DOING?** resonates with ASK FOR IT? Again, Mohamed starts off with the refrain introducing every stanza of the piece. The refrain poses a question to the reader and brings to the fore the sham and futility of our existence. **DESPERADO** is another of those protest pieces in which desperateness is found everywhere. **WALKING MIND** depicts a persona who oscillates and vacillates between hope and despair. Though the persona's 'mind' is 'wrecked' and 'people's predictions wretched' yet his 'way is carved to power'. The persona in **THE SCHOOL – LORRY PARK CHILD** dovetails the popular narrative on street children and child abuse and child labour. The irony is that everything is happening in the 'city' in the full view of the authorities and very little is being done about it. The 'lorry park child' is smart enough to think 'and dodge' because he has been 'tinged by genes alive to live' even though 'crumbs come late in crack saucers'. The first person narrator is alive with the subject of true love in **THE FINAL LOVE**. The issue of 'love' since the days of Biblical and Quranic fore bearers has always occupied centre stage. 'Love' has been characterised by 'loyalty in deception' even though 'preaching folks did not tire'. 'Mankind' is said to have 'extraordinary hypocrisy' and this sends a chilling signal across the poem because where there is no truth then falsehood will prosper. **SISTER** is a highly stylized and economical poem. The diction is sparse yet the message is strong. The assurance and affirmation in the first line gives way to doubt in the second line of the first stanza. Mohamed via his persona is trying to tap into the current discourse women's marginalization and empowerment. The poem **IS YOUR LIFE EVER LOST?** is one of those engaging pieces that inspires in spite of the obvious challenges. It attempts to trivialize suffering on this earth especially so if the suffering were in furtherance of higher righteous ideals. The rewards, as implied by the persona, will be great in the year after. Mohamed Bangura reminds us of the hereafter in **REMEMBER THIS QUESTION?** The piece is very short yet overladen with profound messages. The nearness of the end resonates strongly in this poem. The stanzaic couplets contain two questions and two instructions. **THE SAVIOURS** is not unlike **REMEMBER THIS QUESTION?** The two poems are cut from the same cloth i.e. scriptural or theological poetry. The 'Saviours' are really what mankind needs to make it through in the hereafter. The scourge of the 21st century is laid bare in **EVEN THOUGH IN POVERTY**. The scar on the conscience of humanity as Tony Blair once puts it is still alive today. This poem brings home the pain that is 'poverty', the stress that is 'poverty', the 'hell fire in the heart' that is 'poverty' and the 'enemy pelting' that is 'poverty'. **FASTING** is drawn from the same cloth just like **SAVIOURS** and **REMEMBER THIS QUESTION?** Mohamed reminds us about the power of 'fasting'. It is in the 'scriptures' thus incumbent upon the pious to observe it. 'Fasting' is seen as the 'soul window', eternal salvation fall' and responsible our 'resting in paradise orchards'. 'Fasting is a painful process because of the 'infidels' taunts', 'clipping desires', and the fact that 'tummies empty on banquet'. **TO THE MESSENGER'S CHARACTER** is drawn from the same cloth just like **FASTING, SAVIOURS** and **REMEMBER THIS QUESTION?** Mohamed reminds us about the character of the Prophet Muhammad (S.A.W). The Messenger's character is 'extraordinary in Holy Spirit', 'honest to faith', 'his soul a spotless Angel' and 'modest in appearance', 'soft spoken' and 'master of character'. **I AM NOT IN YOU** is boastful and arrogant piece in the mould of Soyinka's **ABIKU**. The persona's arrogance comes through very strongly. The subjective narrator can neither be held back nor restrained. **DISAPPEARNACE IN NYANGA HILLS** is a typical protest poem in which the persona brings to the fore the challenges and excitement of being abroad in this case Zimbabwe. However, Zimbabwe could be symbolic which means it can represent overseas in relation to the point of extraction. **IN CONVERSATION WITH MY SOUL** is a deeply philosophical piece that hovers between the physical and the virtual. We notice a 'lonely weary' persona being hooked to social media in which his 'heart a tavern' to the point he is 'missing' himself. We are assured by the persona that he does not need a 'hug' since his 'soul is clammy' to him. This piece is very dense and versification lends more weight to its heaviness in terms of subject and style. In a nutshell the piece focuses on technology, religion and the desire to liberate ourselves and walk a fine line. **TALKING BOAT** evokes a sense of drama on the perilous or 'deadly' seas or oceans and rivers across the country. The boats are normally overcrowded and poorly equipped to deal with the elements as they race from 'coast to cope as the sun' sets. As the boats and their passengers travel it is possible they might not get to their destinations. This piece reminds the reader of the struggles of the protagonist in Hemingway's 'Old Man and the Sea' and Melville's 'Moby Dick'. For the Mohamed, the struggles of the persona are very localized and miniaturised compared to the leviathan proportions dealt with by the heroes of Hemmingway and Melville. The piece in its rawness appears inaccessible in terms of style and diction. A lot of symbols have been employed by the poet to capture the readers' imagination as the sojourn begins at Moa-Wharf and ends at the unknown destinations. It is a run of crimes and anxiousness that put the reader on the edge. Mohamed has evoked a stylized visual by capturing both the 'horizon' and 'vessel'. **THE MOON** is drawn from the same cloth just like **FASTING, SAVIOURS** and **REMEMBER THIS QUESTION?** Mohamed reminds us about the power of prayers as heralded by the 'moon' in the greater battle of good over evil in which good must triumph. The persona comes across as undecided with regards his faith and secular pleasantries. The persona is troubled because he 'drenched in … sleep as early as Fitri prayer'. It is hard to believe that the persona is reluctant to shake off yester night sleep. Even his 'mum' protests his disobedience. With reluctance the persona wakes up trembling 'of invisible things' he does not 'bear'. The piece is preoccupied with the morning battle which every prayerful Muslim will contend with as Fajr prayers enter. We are reminded that during this primitive battle 'time' flows inexorably.

This debut collection can safely take its place among the contemporary Sierra Leonean poets like Coker, Gibril, Gbanabom, Farouk, Sheikh Umarr Kamarah, Walon-Jalloh, Kainwo and the others.

ENDORSEMENTS

"Waves of a Raining Mind" is a poignant anthology veering into multifaceted themes. In it, the mundane complex and hilarious merge; yet like immiscible liquids they exude their individual effects. Bangura has been able to bring to life brief encounters, life glimpses and vestiges of history to weave a captivating collection. You are assured of a powerful read.

Ambrose T . Rogers
Department of Language Studies
Fourah Bay College, University of Sierra Leone

***

In his allusive and metaphorical "Waves of a Raining Mind", Mohamed Bangura weaves scenes, characters and experiences into his breathtaking collection of poems that reveal his big heart capable of reaching out to children, beggars and the underprivileged, even as he cements his relationship with the educated and fellow writers. If the underprivileged and voiceless are searching for a champion of their cause; if nature is searching for someone to sing her praises; if education and religion are searching for someone to trumpet their virtues, the search stops with the poems in this collection.

Mrs. Elizabeth Lucy Alberta Kamara
Head English Language Unit
Department of Language Studies
Fourah Bay College, University of Sierra Leone

POEMS →

THE PULSE OF KROOBAY

Up the hill wastes push down to mammoth rest
As cone pigs' baggage canoe to tunnel west
And seems a ship on 'Samba'; so gush
More flow than the rain flush
 Revengeful than the 'Samba' crushes
For enrolling in its trenches
To squashy debris apt slowly
Of collar roofs join to sea molly
Striking cloud stare length fire dearly

Abhorred, as children bed songs vanish
And muddy coal trunk the blanket walls
The playgrounds colored foot bare scorns
As motionless, roads and life toast no coin
  Feeling ignored, forcing migration to unknown

Of lips ashore stutters the gad fly
Hell loose to face judgement unheard
With insignia upward pact debarred
But every breath obey to passion crimes
As beauty prostrate to splendor flames
Lock in cradle fascinated by sunrise trace
Stern stained, eternal as the hen to the chick grace
Or steer pulses mystery truly deface

DUNIA

Awake all horns of my heart!
My heart needs your unity
Toil in fruitful chains
Chains of bamboo in hammock dens

My heart takes the place it deserves
Lead woman of choice to converse
Lightness in front tempting
Rolls of joy in pollen grains
From Mount Athens
To Aberdeen white mansion sorrow
Sprout of road bumps given grey hair tomorrow

My heart toil so fast
But step no rest
My walk so dumb
Ear so numb
My drum not heard afar
But my work child patient

My heart pinned to the mountain
In deep mist strained in guiltless curtain
I pry more in forest to cut the devil's scuffle
Pending all scourges of straw
My heart in the crescent of Dunia need no stray

FREETOWN ABERDEEN WHARF

An Island on heritage
Lifeless as fete wind on river flow
The forests overlook the ocean lights
Land shelving away from the 'Sapes'

In canoes the fish chase
In net the monster head dry and choose
In rag wrappers the hut providers' rush with tongue cajoles
Of heady emotions boil in cackles
Who is to decode that torrent?
The creepy silky mouthy serpent torment

Your price on your beauty
Nothing gain on duty
Homes go empty
An Island in the Ibos remnant style
Calling the 'Sapes' strangers
The 'Sapes' algae first grow here
A plant that suck salt to hear

Where are the 'Sapes' in these mangroves?
Spice of this land withering waves
In the grave yard 'Sapes' stumps are weeds
Cultural bundles are charred in beads
A mark of panicky superstition in large minds
Aberdeen Wharf a habitat of meteors ocean toys

Waves of a Raining Mind / Mohamed Bangura

THE MORNING BIRD'S SONG

Why do I wake to hear creaking fire fly
Risen feverish cold the redden sky
In peep window breezing pinholes heat
With torch flocking the sofa bitter
Not overflowing the Azan's welcome pry

The foggy Harmattan, the cloudy silver linen
The sparrows that warble sweet
Their final love innocence greet
With my eyes looking wide and dripping to say
Is this a day without a song?
The morning birds beaming smile

The morning bird's song reminds me
Of one shaky office joy
Its poor sighs naked gently annoy
Blown up incessant sad hope
Of change smeared dope
A bustard with slacken common grey sense
Alas! A spell epitaph waiting on deserted fields

LINES TO A POST EBOLA POET
(Dedicated to comrade Poet Abdulai Walon Jalloh – Lecturer, Linguistics Unit Fourah Bay College)

Seen from the shadow, when puns dim his forehead
Glued verses wave rafters wing
Of pure discipline the heart to imagery sting
Cheering meekly this dust that follows his wind
Where secret spurs felt the sojourned mind
Ever haste, invoking cliché late to keep the race lost
Muttering chant retiring on that bounty gold coast post

Our joys, our dreams, our passion the bliss
Seated ever to keep pouring in Sophocles
In breaking silence now unfold discourse
Pressing the dew to punch me upraising
To escape the chant spirit debasing
With that taunt of poetic nesting
Attuned elbow treasured friendly circus

Oh! Ruffled, aging the fortune castle manhood
As abject cares bids the kids rattling childhood
Rebuked the faults insular knees
Pipes empty to the sea leafy fleas
I have the stead that listen your shade
Of diction unknown ending in upgrade
Aside the path of sublime lyrics gains

WRITER'S BLOCK

My right hemisphere has gone on vacation
I am neither foresighted nor Narrow - minded

I read Amiri Baraka's poetry in puritan state of serenity
At night he enters my sleep and says
At last, I get to tempt up your brain!

The study table has got recess for weeks
In jealousy of the radio
The electricity reparation is still ongoing

I knock my head with a dagger pencil
Coz nothing good come in utensil
No light is no light and darkness is darkness
In an illusion opposing my poetry composition
Vexed in venom to lay off this verses
This entanglement clipped me kaput!

THE FERRY THAT BROUGHT ME

Amid the ears that came with my luggage
Behind me are old slave remains and distance penury
Stench slums and shackle cubicles startled my admiration
Of suffering hills yawning for their conviction

I am not stripped of my reflection post
In thoughts deepening vein ambition lost
Like a star daubed with cloud linings
My lips stutters when I speak of that crude crossing
'Borbor', the blood genre in my neurons felt the fancy of death

As I imagined where I left my heart
I felt not inspired of my Trace
With the truth of fainting eyes revealing themselves
And my old grand mama became weary grace
Even as I anoint her with my tales

How do I compel the mind of the ferry that brought me here?
Now that the future walking head high
On this bridge that connect my late ancestral fry
Twisted as I hold my monarch goodness I

THE BEACH WAVES

Waves of bleak future
Hugged to each other in torture
Spitting hard milk brink late
Sniffing dust all mourn and dusk beat to beat

Hang up thirst
Drinking sham
Lost in hard honey
Fire dot fire
Nature fights back
Doggy, boo – doggy

The shattering beach waves
Clamped on deaths
Blind lightning speaks tide
Rushing shawls to reside
The day's appetite to decide
Spoon in spoon all lost

IN SEARCH OF MY TEENAGE LOVE

All hopes, joys full in stirred passion
Whatever frame buttered concoction
Feed my lingering armed statue
Reflect the twist of burning desires
And that for down memory lane
Stood Maria's bosom happy in years

I dodge in the back yard
Fading the ward eyeing hard
To arrive with the dole long thoughts
Just in crown felt delights
I flirt slow to woo the feeling posh worn
To listen there the girl soft torn

I kept my mum's purse open
For the kind arms ever blush
All are but coils of chic kiss
With falling thighs modest lush

The dimples grow in eternity
I call a song to the story of vanity
Gasping the dream of long fading touch
Upon this I tell the moon scene couch

COMMON COMRADES

Ah the last fading call returns in 12 years of vernal semesters
And all the glory, that Wisdom tree and 'Bustik' glamour prompters
The rose –beards on music whisper yearning fist brains
Of ceaseless and stress swells faint caress
A dream recalled in lost dream careless
Of old tides born obedient to the leaders burst
Like trail of ant linked in migratory birds' choir

Comrade of the sages! And strategist of the Progress
Into my heart have I dwelt that common sense
More than stories reveal able within the pint
Thoughts all too brash for fun
Of smiles and housemaids fears
Lighten the instructor self- determined gears

Of more than insinuated distant whim
Amid misers punched social sense vital breathings outcry fumbles
Where contract in all her banks laid doubles
Is visible, or schemed on the draft table
A song sung intra and Diaspora companion fuels
Who defrocks candle pour mild thunder?
Rekindling pangs of camaraderie borne in almond wreaths

Dear common room comrades, where is the sweet scent of Home

Waves of a Raining Mind / Mohamed Bangura

Like a wife and water whirlwind strength
Into the darkness the bar calls more for the tar bumps
The moral truth the road needs no rhyme
Tickled in dart of last wine
A hard beneath sense spread so hailed

SWIMMING FISH

A fish swimming beside me on the beach
Snatched away every flap of my feet
And I shone like a shark could not pitch
My dress with pinholes could lead!

I crossed the waves
Emptied the wet proof
Stunned in the sun of dove
And what did I beget:
a woman girly, slumbering on my littering mat

I dusted myself in the mirror of joy
As wails of love with no coy
Under the roofs of noisy palm tree
Hasting to dash home in dews of traffic free
Save the barren crowd measuring pace
Half being turn loveless countenance
Vanished to the ocean boardwalk spectacular

HOME COMING

Coming back from the damn humming Diaspora
McDonalds on one side of liberty
Foo – foo on the other side of 'Mabela'
I am pawning my credit card to uncle Tom
To peel off the shackles of the blacksmith
That tickles me every hour

I trust my ex-ancestors may come back from the evil forest
And think I have been unfaithful to my siblings
That they would not even ask why I have gone to peddle ice cream
On the streets of Washington

With Thomas Dela Rue papers that drives me nut
Only if I know what Uncle Tom thinks of my daughter
I would have stayed to keep myself better
In trust of Diaspora forever demeaning

Waves of a Raining Mind / Mohamed Bangura

HYSTERIA

The grassy fields drizzling afar
Then the dizzy squirrels and jabbering parrots
And after that the drought of rain
That was how solemn life transplant seek
In the dark night, yawning pens blocked before
Speaking the Life is Good pictures flash
Winking the lids cornea bright shadow dash

The light went off
And the dog childless barks fading
The driving vehicles and cars tiring pass
The locks of the gates break farce
In everything went to the fear of other beings in company

Joyous mood flags destiny
As all to join a swam of witty
 Passed the tribal street paddy
Our tight parley decodes the stamped cup cohorts
In line of the week visit prayers
Get- together to know ourselves better

In front the professors passionate stem
Calming the days burden
Cautious to drench in trance
The hollow of the brain fills with yeasty numbers
The outside wind flogging gently
The bar tenders late hour's frustration
To keep bottles dancing on the Davidson Nicol hand

MORE TIME ON THE STOOL?

More time on the stool?
With you by my side
Thumbing my head
Your silvering arm round my shoulder
Reading my folder
Your polished stiletto
Beaming the sky
Oh, freedom!
Don't cuddle me again under this scorching sun

More time on the stool?
Talk to me in absence
Your Photo of presence
Your eyes steering at me
Oh, justice!
Let your way be spoken

More time on the stool?
In a meeting with you
Say your opinion
Your hands are shivering
Picking everything from me
Oh, corruption!
Why is life like this?

More time on the stool?
In discourse to save my country
In a banquet to end the candies

Say your last word
Time is limited
Oh, election!
Choose the angel that you love most

I WILL BECOME A CHILD AGAIN

I will become a child again
My diaper braced up
I will let my mum feed me up
I will let my curly hair grow bushy
Like the intensity of her suckling breast
That held between my face and my handy vest

As I near my weaning time
I will resist the corn pap deception
Like a homesick peasant falling aloud
Of grin pepper smeared to keep me absent mind
My mother's chest the red line
A bastion of hope the last Benny-mix drop
There will I watch as I plant the morning crop

LOVE LATECOMER

Love latecomer
Absent to night to know the least
Dressed in cap turn beast
Emotion at bay
In your eyes
In your foot walk
In your walking arms
Or right here where I am scribbling
Or here where my gift is waiting
Oh, the lane corner shimmering flings!
Love miscreant touch overturns your lips
Like a fire coal shawl that drenches in the raining season

DREAM

In devil silence you sneak in my slumber
And brought pellets to your number
You changed to a mason with shadow of trumping mansions
And this brought stained wealthy manners
As if no sack of joy with your donor
Save the bitterness we battle for favours

The silence of a beam streaming like a grape
I followed your steps to enjoy the bite
In this masking eye play of certainty
Your sight stings the doors of bounty

In doubt I dwell that sad rush
Saddled in counting what I wish
Profane a path I choose with you
Of what you cannot offer
Oh; my hands double thunders
Lost in ploy of rain blunders
Only to bridge in a real world asunder
Take not my belongings as we return!

TUTORS

Tutors
Tuition
You mean journalists?
Mind controllers
You say you
As in roasted strollers

You mean ideal travelers?
Donator's beginners
Sacrificial lambs
Delusion frowns

You mean what?
Tuition
When pay comes ages
When coin stay nut edges
A call to debtors smudges

No need to stay here!
Where?
That room of noise
No one to hear
It darkens the path dear
Lightness in brightness
Wish of all

Ask not for food?
No coin here
Dream ends in the air

Waves of a Raining Mind / Mohamed Bangura

Dust shadow man
Victim of wisdom mourn
Thoughts not useful
Aspires more
Don't tell that to kids sure
Tutors' gone manure

Waves of a Raining Mind / Mohamed Bangura

TO MY POETRY MENTOR

I imagined a poetry mentor I cannot see
When my mind in strangled cables fee
Clung grievous feed roared guru of vocals
In the Diaspora flowered dared wit
But slow as he was calm to ever talk
Made me inspired and walk
He lives in revolutionary Africa as he lived in the Newfoundland Aztecs

My poetry is naked as I gaze him sit
So my heart pleased whenever he seep
My knowing of him is forever picturesque
So is my buddy admired and grotesque

In question we pray him more
In reply he said it sure
His insight dazzles the cubs
His poetry your diagnosis tubs
His poetry not in his neurons!
His fancy lost our grey matter
All is not sheltered to alter

His face of poetry light reflect my tap of words
As I scribbled faster than my fashion could fads
His poetry my poetry of romance
Poetry mentor be lodged in span
You could get that oubliette fan
Not to your poet conscience palliative
My poetry mentors my inventiveness

KENEMA

I sang you a song
You gave me 'Simbeck'
I brought you ascending wonders
You showed me floral paradise
I lift the 'Kamboi' to you
You hug me with scenic acacia trees

I may not tell in cave rocks
Mourning smell pours freshness
Plucks of wild fruits send tears of dimness
Kenema where do you live?
The dusty tarmac
'Bojelah' river flows
You bask in hoping arms
Kenema your ante I share

My tongue tied in your speech
Kenema am I like you?
But in vision darkness your illumination voiceless
The meals served in your name
Panicked my trimmed shirt in the face of shame
I tried to be the same
Kenema dragged every fingers of my novel
In your seeds I polished my navel
So fulfilled to watch crescent and stars

THE KALAHARI

Languishing daily chores of spirituality
Affixed my body temperature
With parching birds busy in their picks
Busy within their spirits

I want to take a picture
Keeping my tourist lens could be perfect store
For all I want to show

In the beauty of those plummeting feathers of theirs
Hit by the cold and dusty Kalahari Desert
With trails of bush men like lions trail
The beauty of nature's nail
I can't wait to unveil

ON THE GRAVE OF A WAR HERO

On the grave of a war hero
Lions and hyenas play on this grave
Leopards tickle their peers
Fox and elephants sleep on this grave
Cook their prey there
Summon their meeting here
Fight for invading untamed kinds

On the grave of a War Hero
Monkeys sing and form a rude choir
Birds serve as letter experts
Poultry writing are seen all over as epitaph
Spiders built their stunning mansions up there
The grave janitor had no option
He had to take this action
 To invite all and sundry
Only to say to the gathering of all
This grave is a warrior's place of rest!

THE HARMATTAN

A cotton blanket that covered itself to the end of the country
 Fighting with all things visible
Why should this be a duel with our lips and skin?
With a single toast of wind from 'Targrin'
Arrived angels of tropical misty snow
 We are lost in the hole of a needle blow
Why is this happening to us?

When the Vaseline stood its grounds to save the situation
Shaking our trembling veins in the aberration
And bathing the cold uncertain force
At last the sun intervenes in our call
I maul the Harmattan with my stockings and jackets.

But yet not too strong to speak with no chimney's air
Are we turn into planetary beings with whiteness
As we speak and touch water
Of flora and fauna smashed to this grandmaster

THE FIRST SUN OF THE DRY SEASON

It is better to chill out again in hustle
To be at some 'Ataya' base cocoon
And keep the youthful exuberance double
For when it takes root
Life finds oppression eating our peanut blind foot
The last man standing air maestro seems persuasive
We long to learn the language of the dungeon
Even a dog barking ascent sounds meaningful
And what have you on your table?
Only the roast meat sticks crumble
Out the first sun of the dry season

FOURAH BAY COLLEGE LIBRARY

Astound for sure what brought me here
Or what I was looking for years
As I hurried past the index cards
On the first shelves and return sections
It was as if I had turned into a weevil
In panoply for a log to feast

Fuming concrete pesticide my mind
My quest beat to the zest
Cordoned like the sight of an Ebola crest
I dropped fears on my trail

In the Africana Collection
I leafed through serial reference books
As if I was slowly drowsing
I looked around for a water bed
But fate has it done the gem fed
For braving the hegemony of the brainiest

The reading room was lukewarm
I could hear podium chants
Mohammed Ali was talking black power to Malcolm X
In a loud voice while reading poems with Amir Baraka
In solitary Langston Hughes scribbling with Ezra Pound
Where is the comradeship of the elegiacs?
Of ideas sold to the dusty cost
Or death taken it toll lost!

THE HOUSE IN THE FOREST

The sun burns it
The rain baths it
The wind calls it to a meeting
In the presence of yelling vultures
The night advice it to be calm
And consoles it with nature solitary
The dumb house that begets the forest

The animals begs it for food
The owners replace it
The hunter past within without noticing
In the midst of smelling meats
And saliva is gone to roost
Creeping the house that begets the worst

DISTANT SCHOLAR

Wandering off my task
Influenced my stocks
A step of consensus
That receives my admiration

From hills and muddy roads
Puffed in sweat and laughter
My hands are empty
Sleeping thoughts bitten by bounty
I cannot sense because I am incensed
My joy of home keeps haunting
Of not only witty but my dream of a distant scholar
With the instinct of a perceiver
 Reaching a bumper merger

Here I am in that dream of a man
Botched by probation in gratis
Wanting to stay till manna combs
I have great hope in that mount that made crumbs
My mountain of farfetched pervasion
A wandering mood my state of aspersion
In reflection of bashful material boom

BEAUTIFUL ORCHARD

It may glue my zest as I brood here
With note of all unknown smell to me
Lost in deep mind in happiness fresh feel
And fruits and trees sandwich the path I follow
Talks of nature pumps the love I glow

When all beside was deaf
So let me be, and if the forest wild whistle
I will be in mute cocoon bristle
Adamant to cave the butter fly gentle brute
Reciting a child mourn prayer to fickle

Embrace me with taste unbroken sequence
Fear of no sound fearful beast
Gazing motionless of fire flies sight
Of seconds, seconds overturn the fright
Unfettered ghost heard unharmed
I trust the beauty of nature to pelt
Wash off the challenge task watching the sky line
The baskets of breasted foliage arrive placed
The reecho of stories over gossip

Waves of a Raining Mind / Mohamed Bangura

THE MYTH COTTON TREE

Strained in the myth of Kith and Kin
Of drums dripping and dare
Of what no dogma has borne
Of hardly what eyes could surf
Of mystery huts erected in that myth tree

Locked in brawling ideas
Monster spirits dwells with all exegesis
 What ordinary 'Hindolos' and 'Hingas' concocts in vain
 Witches and wizards in joyful pain
 Murky hawks that has dozens of swine
 Cradle babies' purges sacrificial pulpits vine
 And owls singing in nomenclature denture

Myth cotton tree can't you parley this image?
'Ndo - mamakumeisias' reject you bowing bondage
Extraordinary you are in ancestral pottery
We speak of 'Honamuis', 'Kolokotos' to exit your sultry
Stunning eyes gather your fall

Your fall predicts imminent deaths
Deaths of twin cutters
Lost buckets of insinuated palace attendees of yours
Travelling to Fouta of 'Kugbays' and 'Kurgbas'
Ruins of ghost yard temples
Cotton tree you still a lion's dreams myth
Fidelity giant gone desperate mythical

LAUGHTER

A journey of laughter
Prays in the counter
Laughter of immense taunter
In that playful twilight fever
In the name of 'Gewo' dosed ever

Keeping prayer to that force of the forest woods
The woods that listen in the wind
As the wind skipped
So the trees skin ripped
Roped in that body

When in something with no cover
In life comes the mind
Locked in constant distance
 Flogged in destiny

A destiny of indifference and uncertainty
Clogged in mystery humpty
Hooked in midnight prostration
With hope resurrecting itself as it did before
Laughter romanced humanity
Bitter as the heart dignity

EDUCATION

Education
This sculptor of man
World key
Minds touch
Man's manual
The way to righteousness

Education
Path full of thorn
Sand covered
Rugged tides

The hour of brown study
The night of sacrifice
Sitting, still   till
Candle's eye drops last tear
Till lamps light dry
Till bulb tire
Still, till, till
Put not thoughts to rest

THE CLASS ROOM IS A MOTHER

The class room bending show of abstractions
Children fight for its bounds of possessions
Others place a call in material gains
Kicking notions that profit the head

The world is troubled when your name is mentioned
I grab my hands with the touch you pat me
When I was casual in eating mine
A home that nothing has ever conquered
As if set explosion of illiteracy is a weakling

Oh; beauty that beauty could birth in words
Will my heart be the same?
In memory of the bliss dripping my glad tidings
The cool silence upward the brains gliding's
God! Change the music, like the sound of my childhood seal
Preserved the rain that the nation's pacific could not fill

SUN SET ON THE SHORE

Wow, what is that blessed ocean liner beaming
To this dusk hour of the day's shrill breath
The ships crosses to that cunning Bay
To appease the late-blooming jetty
And this wailing market shields
Which only just turned a deserted field

To the curved canoes hoisting overboard
To cajole the shawl that brings wealth pest
Don't squeeze up wait to hear the banks blast
The rushing kingfisher adieu to rest
And the sigh of a mystery still feels chest

Ah what is that blessed darkness plight
To this late hours of the jolly night
The clubs poised to open ancestral discs
And the wave of a fisher man leaves
Alas! Dodging myself styled imagination
A wealthy pile of fins dangling faces
On that sun set on the shore

THE GRASS AND I

This rabbit where did it come from?
On the squirm of your blazer
And me where I stumble as you relieved
In your voice did I lose myself.

This grass when did it take this journey
The first diamond drop your passage
And then teach my lips the unknown.

Child, something must have happened or not
For you to toy the aged rough your future
And console the bickering cradle
Haughty sounds and fatigue scramble
This grass,   the rabbit's tail and I

WOMAN STAND UP

Rise up Rosa Parks
Your kids call!
Where are your wombs?
I see no chest so big
As pain clenched your smile
I swear unto you- that I shall listen when you
Begin to call us to this lead!

Rise up Maya Angelou
Your midwives call!
Where are your napkins?
I see no face that did not see your care
I swear unto you-that we shall milk your breast
When you bring poetry to rest
Lapping on your wrapper's quest

Rise up Ella Koblo Gulama
Your 'Salone' calls!
Confused as fate befalls the 'Ojah'
Shall the 'OJah' live as cooks or now leaders?
That's the question - choose your `50/50'!
Advocates of Sierra Leonean women
I vow unto your presence   to choose this voiced path
I swear unto you that benchers the 'Ojah' shall no longer be!

PITY

Shout your heart high
Blink and don't shun I
Dance your fingers
Wait and get me my dress stringers
Blah, blah and blah, but
And choose my sea hut
Take a step
Run and arrive when your mum disappears
Swim your lap
But save me the last clap

Waves of a Raining Mind / Mohamed Bangura

WHY BLAME ME?

Why blame me as blame sees me not
I am the blame that is not blame
But you see blame in my blame
I escaped the pains of not getting anything
But this nothing is nothingness

I bow in dawn for dusk to change
As filtered in the common inns brethrens rope
Assuring this young chap of soon found hope
In defense to the brim 'Tomby' tree
The devil waves off the future
I prove the devil naked nurture
To reach where comrades have checked denture

I am here to stay as divinity stood more divine
To leg padding my own drones
Of no drone muscle this drone
Why blame me?
I am the innocent blame
Not as your folks spike!

DRUMS BORN AGAIN

As sorrows ting my dancing head
Underneath the pitch of calling goers feast stead

The day's drums speak of demons
The demon is judged
Its defense purged
Demon's invisibility echoes the congregation
When the demon speaks, fading drums confess

Will drums be born again?
Where the demons steer
Duels show in the anointing savvy spirit

To sow seeds for future ravages
Belief walks to terraces and slums
Singing away from drums born again
Leaves you dirty vain
Try it never!

THE MEMORY VALLEY

Blazing eyes dodged to the memory valley
A valley of eternal bliss dolly
A valley of promised maiming doom
A calling hope down every line soul

Some choose the balcony to grasp the known
To greet the green packed scenery frown
With ghost squirrel and monkeys showing bumps

Afar the eyes stretched
Living ghost lit up the islands sketch
Island of affluence and tarmac snatch

This valley reminds the ear of a journey
A journey to unknown banquet
What shroud to take to Eve?
Charity hands to ease

I choose to reminisce this valley
I choose to because my spirituality speaks to
This valley knows no young and old
Knows no rich and poor
Knows no humble and haughty
Knows no high and low jaunty
This valley takes my conscience
This valley forever I see

THE EXCESSES OF POLITICS

The excesses of Politics
The excesses of desires
The drowsiness of negligence
The entrance into garbage
Begin with tight fist levity
Few overthrow the majority

The preference of wrong to right
The show of inexpediency
The manipulation of ideas
The opposition to methods
The celebration of generosity
Rough is the guilty

The impetuosity of rancour
Rooted bridge of envy
Rime anger mogul
Lust for power to muzzle
To fleece, to embezzle
No glory to dirty politics!

Over patronizing of the people
Pride of the sun and the palm tree
The humiliated masses fade
Punched in their shade
The excess of politics
A checked slavery!

IGNORANCE

Ignorant path in vain
Late to arrive in heaven
Gnarled and braced leaven
With stale meat stomach weary

In ignorance
Folks applaud and suffer
Masked and duped
Smeared and reared

In ignorance we scorned everything
When infallibles exist!
Lion fox   roam on the command of the street
To prey on its teeth

In ignorance
Thought twist in sly
Vultures fly high
Fluttering wings to keep well
Be not staked swell
Folks! In ignorance still
Ignored   forever!

WAITING TIME

Waiting time!
Of days ruined in excitement
Losing direction of cause
And causing disenchantment vile

Waiting time!
School folks in pangs of surprise
Admiring this time and lost in deprive
Comrades' feet stern like an eagle's flight
Searching for that lust new romance
Disappearing in no sense of nuisance
The regret of an odd odyssey
Waiting time could not be waiting fruit
Tempting shadows of roughness
Dangling heart like rose pollen toughness
Lodged in doubts and frustration
Heading nowhere in mutation

Waiting has no path waiting
Eyes tumbling here and there
From the mind calls love hugs of old and young hogs
Riding the edges of life
Waiting time awaits no waiting
Let us trap life in the velvet

Smiling folks of ugly cogs
Driving the well thoughts mentor
Arriving at the cross roads
Dating his common sense to the gutters

Waves of a Raining Mind / Mohamed Bangura

Gutters of the Hoipolois domain
Waiting the awakening is awaiting disdain

ASK FOR IT?

Ask for it?
The week comes with it
When?
The office day
The busy bazaar
Busy within them

Ask for it?
Sold just now
Not seen in the dark days annoy
Hot stuff
Heated march
Wait the next day

Ask for it?
An aisle of   difference
Money candies
Reading to sleep
With honey cream
A Peep to double ream

Ask for it?
Surprise!
Entice!
Hard to call; only beam
Hard to cultivate
Call of the illiterate

Waves of a Raining Mind / Mohamed Bangura

Phonetics a puzzle
Ask for it in baffle?
A bird said it is there

BEGGARS

Beggars in pain!
Standing
Pushing
Rushing
Sitting
Crawling

To put away starving days
Waiting drops of coins
Quick silver papers
No one cares
Others frowned and smacked
Some hissed and spat
The gentry's hand short

Few are excited
Rains are dejected
Choose not the evil path
Nature decides
Folks reside
Hope presides
Soon! Soon!
Tomorrow   the better

Waves of a Raining Mind / Mohamed Bangura

WHAT ARE WE DOING?

What are we doing?
Don't ask!
Screaming
Shouting
Humming
Drumming in the news room

What are we doing?
The mouse clicks
More pages today
No time to stay
Little to say
Less to pay
Go home the same

What are we doing?
Work done so crazy
Pitching everything
Wrong something
Do anything
Bring nothing

What are we doing?
You know!
Next bird nest
More flocks to cage
Lion food to serve
More snap to make eyes show despair

Waves of a Raining Mind / Mohamed Bangura

What are we doing?
Don't ask!
It's a drown
Where?
Say it there

DESPERADO

Desperado in the yard
Desperate in the dock
Cum like moose
Charged in pose
Locked in dose
Creak and buzz

Desperado in love
Angry move
Shrewd housemaid
Irrational cloak
Torn, tort, tooth

Hope dashed
Step in cold
Who to know?
Desperado looks!
The kite flies
In muttering lips
Killing memories
Raping privileges
Desperado knowledge
Clipped College

Who to blame?
You tell it to the hyenas
In slums
In shackles
On the groove

Waves of a Raining Mind / Mohamed Bangura

Allow us to eat sand!
Where we go your soul don't go
Drought can't sell
Promise worst
Thorny cook
Miscreant hook
Information deferred! Harped! Harped!

WALKING MIND

My walking mind is wrecked
People's predictions wretched
Your way is carved to power
Mild toast of thorny way to keep my mind
My mind's desire missing my old mind
Is my old mind in serious vegetables?
It's a game to my comrades

My walking mind from a shadow
Full of bout
Mixed with doubt
Mind set of minds
My mind is safe
Making my kidney in gaffe

My mind in breeze
Draw smiles
Tailored more idleness
Smiling mind to other minds
Thinking wombs
Reaping the dwarf's olive
Kicking the lanterns of their mind

My mind in departure
Let me be not that fracture
My mind with pals
Locking my mind with dancing dolls
Do not fall!
Your mind could lift you

Waves of a Raining Mind / Mohamed Bangura

Your exchanges is hilarious
Dreaming my mind in you
Trust with pebbles in the cave
Never stop my mind shave!
My mind travels in shadows

THE SCHOOL - PARK CHILD

A child in the city
Lost in hard labour consciousness
With signs admired and identified

Slow to follow
Sure to thought and dodge
Tinged by genes alive to live
The advocate mother relieve
Abusers smiles in rough waters
Crumbs come late in crack saucers

Another day is back with trays in bus parks
Levering customers in close eyes
The magic of profit and sale
All is done!
Rush home for more

The School Park – child bring in grades
With no study
A reflection of surprise
The way forward to sunrise

Dull bones could not respond
As the young mind is weak lying underbids
With visit to cookery
A strength of pills in others stomach
What the difference?
Same path to suffering
Suffering has no substitute

Waves of a Raining Mind / Mohamed Bangura

Only substitute of swords in that sight
That sight of curse in doing the street
The school park – child the fright

THE FINAL LOVE

In my first life of yester long
Wanders up a bit in arms
The end of alms
Purity babbles
Morality bubbles
Universal clarion chores
You get the best

You get the best from mamas
Dying kith and kins
Loyalty in deception
Your daily breast listen perception
Preaching folks did not tire
Step eaves drop of sages' fire
Chastised and shamed

The final love
The link, the spirit
From Adam
To   Hawa
You mean Eve?
A fabric rolled down to generations
Nothing stops
The final love scoops
Mankind extraordinary hypocrisy

What else do we need?
Where a husband worries about family
Where a poetry zoo in solace hung

Waves of a Raining Mind / Mohamed Bangura

Where a college is wronged
Where ethic's abashed
Where a town is robbed
Where a city is in shred
A gift to man in final love cast the end
I don't know!
Ask the clergy?

SISTER

Sister I know;
Sister do you know me
Yet you scorn at me

Sister, I got a sister I said
Sister I pest
Sister in rapt
Tap, tap, and tap;
Rap, rub, and rip
Ram, rim, rain

Sister I know;
Sister, as far as I could bear
Life is getting bare

Sister I know;
I will stay till you care
For all I want to wear
You walk me to fair

Sister I know;
I love my sister and
Let your sister love me
The future holds trust in me

Waves of a Raining Mind / Mohamed Bangura

IS YOUR LIFE EVER LOST?

Ask your life?
That wallows in nature's perfection
The Mover's choice of purity
The Mover's throne the invincible paucity
The pride of bliss in doffing Palms

With your life, you get the just
Humanities trust
All doubts cast off
Patience mother
Soft daughter
Obedience choice
Nursing Spring guarding Voice

Is your life ever lost?
Where homes in spiritual hunger
Where beauty is peel off
Where the treasure of womanhood is first of
Where veils are shamed in ignorance
Where is your life?
Her image is painted in your strive

In her name we celebrates
In memories of heavenly debate
The curtain is up
Humanity! Settle down for grace
Open your arms to embrace

Waves of a Raining Mind / Mohamed Bangura

Is your life ever lost?
Your life is here least!
Take your golden place in our hearts

Waves of a Raining Mind / Mohamed Bangura

REMEMBER THIS QUESTION?

Remember yourself this question?
 Answer it here because the grave is near

When in the grave?
Pinned this in your shy way

Remember yourself?
Remember your direction
Remember your path leave your pride

Remember yourself?
Need your scale
Remember your burden gain you success

THE SAVIOURS

Master of Godly favours
Blessed is the igloo of the saviours
Prayer of wanton forbearance
Blessings from limitless tolerance
Of families in purity

Blessings abound!
The message in no turning back mission
 Bells the right path and truth fruition
Incredible from the invincible portion

With illumination derived from divine vine
O f unschooled and womb dine
Blessed possessions
Confessed professions
Blessings forever
The saviors' mandates the everlasting

EVEN THOUGH IN POVERTY

Even though poverty is painful
Painful to mull, stressful
Dumping its pains in the farms
Poverty is hell fire in the heart
An enemy pelting to destroy

Nothing on mama's hand
Even though her hands are free
To live for it
To stand against it
To wait not for it
Even though in poverty is death

FASTING

Spirituality lodged in all scriptures
For the righteous to obey
Infidels' taunts
Brush down hunts
Solemn shadow
Piety of the soul window

Fasting culled slit bones
Dying call
Rush of all
Hasty break
Fasting be not surprise!
Ancient Prophets redoubles
Present past call
Eternal salvation fall

Fasting drumming no sins
Clipping desires
Tummies empty on banquet
Assurance cry
Do you hope to see more years in heaven peeling more sins?
Fasting gone from souls
Resting in paradise orchards

TO THE MESSENGER'S CHARACTER

Extraordinary in Holy Spirit words work
As words work wonders
In expectative eyes
Honest to faith

With silky brown pigment
His soul a spotless Angel wore white
 Walks in subtlety full of humbleness
Modest in appearance
Soft spoken radiance
My heart sinks in praise

Coded messages to free humanity
Preserved in the Holy Scriptures sobriety
Impressed sages of all corners
Here is the path
Full of eternal bath
Make your choice!
You are assured
Cast no doubt
The messenger is the master of character

I AM NOT IN YOU

Understand that if you debase love my right
I am not in you sight
I am what you dream not
I am the moon that shouts
Because I know of no out

I am not in you
Why cajole wisdom?
I am wormed in your fear
As you pick the day untold gear

I am not in you
Take me away from your wastefulness
Take it as you select your gladness
Why drag your guidance?
I am not much full
Only warps remain heroes fool
I am not in you like gullible gall

Waves of a Raining Mind / Mohamed Bangura

DISAPPEARANCE IN NYANGA HILLS

Stones crooked footpath palace
Conquered red pygmies of snow solace
Of heroes and heroines wonders flowery tales
The white man's trickery in the winter hales
With silent poison thrilling dales

Here I am in caged irksome dock of martyrdom
In the conscience of my two births
The sounds that re - echoed in the chant of incendiary style Africanism
Wash off in this tide of Zimbabwe's black power
 In revenge of inhuman mortars and pestles
Diary punched fickle the 'Mahehu' corn porridge
The sweet taste of free air is better than haulage

Here I am at Africa University
Intimidated by mould multicultural flags
In the midst of the heat summer blanket
Of Mutare lost to the white man's character!

Nyanga Hills vexed as Leopold Sedar Senghor's negritude
In this hill dwell, trespass nay like the white man fortitude
Nyanga Hill will disappear in rocky steep
Of stories told till of Nyanga's vexation deep
Neglect, Nyanga Hills pathless groove
And waiting deafer more graves

IN CONVERSATION WITH MY SOUL

I am lonely weary
In this occultist technology
When social media the milky orgy
Yet my heart a tavern
I am missing myself
Inviting my soul feels high brow
In conversation with my soul ascends zealots

My soul's company reinvents my humanity
A bilateral mark of my body fruity
I don't need a hug!
My soul is clammy in me

When my soul speaks to the sky
All cease in this friendship
Eternity pumps love limitless
I am when I know
My soul nurtures no hate in this vain life I vow
Is conversation with my soul heretic?
May be the orient turban fox could not hear
My soul is unsung
My soul a galaxy lodged in righteousness

TALKING BOAT

Welcome overcrowding noise
Thought versus inclinations race
Experience a bolt down games
Catch the dope cheats eyes baked
From Mu--wharf to the future harbor
Deadly as the peasants journey
At this stage the worst erupts
There I talk

Coast to cope as the sun set
Inflammable battered pitched distress
My night vision only listens to the alert of our presence
A vessel horizon of sea human poachers
Dosed to unknown swamps ruling the waves
Of water detained as fish fins
Put the lock quickly pregnant as the crew
The gastro fang not spared
There I talk

I tried to find my place
This is not my destination
The fair wind blew, the snow damp show
When looking eastward, I shrink
All the sky lifts at the scorching sun brink
There I talk

About, at bay, in dance into that misty sea
Of evils dreamt at post I sail
Of giants motion breathe as death

Waves of a Raining Mind / Mohamed Bangura

Time after time I crawl
I flip and flap to gain the twist of water swells
The final touch in frustrated spell
Without the wind would I ever sail
There I talk

THE MOON

Drenched in my sleep early as 'Fitiri' prayer steers
Of belief battered the sparks in me
My watchful mum yelled the disobedience
Of the coming sunset curse credence
In those who behold their sleep at the hour dead

Awake drunk in nothing to swallow
Why do I tremble of invisible things I don't bear?
Displayed in many other writings of the cloud
Scribble down in the middle of the night
Fall into poetic lines bite
To break the road swallowed spite
Over the house is narrowed into rude Circle
The edge of its overlooking bright star trickle
The white mass thinning at its edge
Fight with its twinkling brilliance gauge

The moon is out gazing wild into the sky
The cock crow perpetual tune ticking
Sweet I to more sleep condemned
I saw the enclave of my ancestors in story faithful
In lust for the moon I saw a spirit man
In inexorable flow of time
This underlies death mime
All flowing mirroring blaze

Waves of a Raining Mind / Mohamed Bangura

SIERRA LEONEAN WRITERS SERIES (SLWS)

Focusing on academic, fictional, and scientific writing that will complement other relevant materials used in schools, colleges, universities and other tertiary institutions, the Sierra Leonean Writers Series (SLWS) aims to promote good quality books by Sierra Leoneans writing on any topics and other writers from around the world who write on themes and issues about Sierra Leone.

It is the publisher's hope that students and other readers in Sierra Leone will eventually be at least some of the primary beneficiaries of these works. Not only will people in Sierra Leone be able to read materials that relate to their own lives and experiences, budding writers will also be able to draw inspiration from the efforts of their compatriots and other established writers.

Submitted work undergoes a rigorous peer-review process before being accepted for publication, with an international editorial board providing guidance to writers.

SLWS, based in Warima and Freetown in Sierra Leone, distributes books globally through AMAZON.COM. In Sierra Leone, SLWS books are currently available at the SLWS Bookshop in Warima (near Masiaka) and at CLC Bookshop, 92 Pademba Road in Freetown.

SLWS co-publishes some titles with Karantha Publishers in Sierra Leone.

For further information, please visit our website: www.sl-writers-series.org
or contact the publisher, Prof. Osman A. Sankoh (Mallam O.) publisher@sl-writers-series.org

Published Books – a milestone of the 50th title has been reached in September 2016!

1	Osman A. Sankoh (Mallam O.)	2001/ 2016	*A Memoir*	*Hybrid Eyes – An African in Europe*
2	Osman A. Sankoh (Mallam O.)	2001	*Non-fiction*	*Beautiful Colours*
3	Sheikh Umarr Kamarah	2002/ 2015	*Poems*	*Singing in Exile and The Child of War*
4	Abdul B. Kamara	2003/ 2015	*A Memoir*	*Unknown Destination*
5	Samuel Hinton	2003	*Poems*	*The Road to Kenema*
6	Karamoh Kabba	2005/ 2016	*A Novel*	*Morquee – The Political Drama of Wish over Wisdom*
7	Yema Lucilda Hunter	2007	*A Novel*	*Redemption Song*
8	Joe A. D. Alie	2007/ 2015	*Research Text*	*Sierra Leone Since Independence – History of a Postcolonial State*
9	Mohamed Combo Kamanda	2007	*A Play*	*The Visa*
10	J Sorie Conteh	2007	*A Novel*	*In Search of Sons*
11	Michael Fayia Kallon	2010/ 2015	*A Novel*	*The Ghosts of Ngaingah*

12	J Sorie Conteh	2011	*A Novel*	*Family Affairs*
13	Winston Forde	2011	*A Play*	*Layila, Kakatua wan bi Lida*
14	Eustace Palmer Doc P.	2012	*A Novel*	*A Pillar of the Community*
15	Siaka Kroma	2012	*Non-fiction*	*Manners Maketh Man – Adventures of a Bo School Boy*
16	Mohamed Combo Kamanda (ed)	2012	*Short Stories*	*The Price and other Short Stories from Sierra Leone*
17	Sigismond Tucker	2013	*A Memoir*	*From the Land of Diamonds to the Isle of Spice*
18	Bailah Leigh	2013	*Non-fiction*	*Dilemma of Freedom – A Diary from Behind Rebels Lines in the Sierra Leone Civil War*
19	Nnamdi Carew	2013	*A Novella*	*Tiger Fist – Two Stories*
20	Yema Lucilda Hunter	2013	*A Novel*	*Joy Came in the Morning*
21	Ebenezer 'Solo' Collier	2013	*Research Text*	<u>Primary & Secondary Education in Sierra Leone – Evaluation of more than 50 years of</u>

				PRACTICES & *POLICIES*
22	Gbananom Hallowell	2013	*Short Stories*	*Gbomgbosoro - Two Stories*
23	Sheikh Umarr Kamarah & Majorie Jones (eds)	2013	**Poems**	**beg sol noba kuk sup** - *An Anthology of Krio Poetry*
24	Siaka Kroma	2014	*Short Stories*	*Tales from the Fireside*
25	Syl Cheney-Coker*	2014	*Poems*	*The Road to Jamaica*
26	Dr Sama Banya	2015	*A Memoir*	*Looking Back – My Life and Times*
27	Andrew K Keili	2015	*Social Commentary*	*Ponder My Thoughts – Vol. 1*
28	Jedidah A. O. Johnson	2015	*A Novel*	*Youthful Yearnings*
29	Oumar Farouk Sesay	2015	*A Novel*	*Landscape of Memories*
30	Oumar Farouk Sesay	2015	*Poems*	*The Edge of a Cry*
31	Gbanabom Hallowell	2015	*A Novel*	*The Road to Kaibara*
32	Mohamed Gibril Sesay*	2015	*A Novel*	*This Side of Nothingness*
33	Yema Lucilda Hunter	2015	*A Novel*	*Nanna*
34	Yusuf	2015	*Research*	*Development,*

	Bangura		*Text*	*Democracy & Cohesion*
35	Lansana Gberie	2015	*Research Text*	*War, Politics & Justice in West Africa*
36	Yema Lucilda Hunter	2015	*A Biography*	*An African Treasure: In Search of Gladys Casely-Hayford 1904-1950*
37	Moses Kainwo	2015	*Poems*	*Ayo Ayo Ayo and other Love Songs*
38	Abdulai Walon-Jalloh	2015	*Poems*	*Voices and Passions*
39	Gbanabom Hallowell (Ed.)	2016	*Short Stories*	*In the Belly of the Lion – An Anthology of new Sierra Leonean Short Stories*
40	Ahmed Koroma	2016	*Poems*	*Along the Odokoko River - Poems*
41	George Coleridge-Taylor	2016	*A Memoir*	*Transformation in Transition*
42	Karamoh Kabba	2016	*Research Text*	*Fire from Timbuktu: A Dialogue with History*
43	Umu Kultumie Tejan-Jalloh	2016	*A Memoir*	*Telling It As It Was: The Career of A Sierra Leonean Woman in Public Service*

44	Ambrose Massaquoi	2016	*Poems*	*Along the Peal of Drums: Collected Poems (1990-2015)*
45	Mohamed Gibril Sesay	2016	*Poems*	*At the Gathering of Roads (Poems)*
46	Gbanabom Hallowell	2016	*Poems*	*Manscape in the Sierra: New and Collected Poems 1991-2011*
47	Gbanabom Hallowell (Ed.)	2016	*Short Stories and Poems*	*Leoneanthology: Comtemporary Short Stories and Poems from Sierra Leone*
48	Gbanabom Hallowell	2016	*Poems*	*Don't Call Me Elvis and Other Poems*
49	Bakar Mansaray	2016	*Short Stories*	*A Suitcase Full of Dried Fish and Other Stories*
50	Gbanabom Hallowell	2016	*Poems*	*The Art of the Lonely Wanderer*

*co-published with Karantha Publishers

www.ingramcontent.com/pod-product-compliance
Lightning Source LLC
Chambersburg PA
CBHW032145040426
42449CB00005B/413